THAT
THAT

MADE IN MICHIGAN WRITERS SERIES

GENERAL EDITORS

Michael Delp, Interlochen Center for the Arts

M. L. Liebler, Wayne State University

ADVISORY EDITORS

Melba Joyce Boyd
Wayne State University

Stuart Dybek
Western Michigan University

Kathleen Glynn

Jerry Herron
Wayne State University

Laura Kasischke
University of Michigan

Thomas Lynch

Frank Rashid
Marygrove College

Doug Stanton

Keith Taylor
University of Michigan

A complete listing of the books in this series can be found online at wsupress.wayne.edu

POEMS BY KEN MIKOLOWSKI

WAYNE STATE UNIVERSITY PRESS

DETROIT

Published by Wayne State University Press, Detroit, Michigan 48201.

19 18 17 16 15   5 4 3 2 1

ISBN 978-0-8143-4065-3 (paperback)
ISBN 978-0-8143-4066-0 (ebook)

Library of Congress Control Number: 2014953090

Publication of this book was made possible by a generous gift from The Meijer Foundation.
Additional support was provided by Michigan Council for Arts and Cultural Affairs
and National Endowment for the Arts.

Designed and typeset by Bryce Schimanski
Composed in Dante MT

For Wendy and Anton

THAT
THAT

THIS

is

THIS

is too

THIS IS THIS
and that's that

NOT
that that
that that

POEM

you can't just write anything
and call it a poem

BLACK WORDS
surrounded
by white space

ARS NICE POETICA

a poem must be
not mean

SHE THINKS

she has a mind
of her own

GETTING OLD

gets old
real quick

WELL FED

torso

more so

BALD
no more
hair there

VIRGIN

intact
in fact

FAT MAN BLUES

I've grown so lonesome
since my belly's grown some

NO MORE
and
no less

PALINDROME

I love you
you love me

YOU AND ME

and every thing

SOMETIMES

I don't think of you
for hours

POETICS
makes bedfellows
estranged

REALITY
not really

AUTHORITY
never mind

CORN FIELD
each row opens
as you pass by

YOU ARE

what you art

ANYTHING CAN BE ART

not everything is

BRAD

Pitt

NONE

of the above

WATER
drip drop
until not

SANITATION
for the nation

I HAVE
no idea

HOMAGE

I've never met a deadline
I've ever met yet

WHY I AM NOT A NEW YORK POET

Detroit

NOTHING ELSE
but to say that

PERMITTED TO FEEL
they felt

SHORT NOVEL

he always right
she left

LOVE POEM

man

women

THIS IS

a short poem

THIS IS

not a poem

THANK YOU

for not being
an asshole

THOSE THREE LITTLE WORDS

you are drunk

WOULDN'T IT BE WONDERFUL

if the whole thing
were like the good part

STOP ME

if you've heard
this one before

OCTOPUS
rhinoceros

THE MEANING IS SOMEWHERE

so we go everywhere

OUTSIDE

the three month summer dies

YOUR LIP ON IT

is it itself

COME ON

just drop your pants
this ain't romance

SMUT

is just tums
spelled backward

NO MATTER HOW MUCH

they lower the bar in poetry
I always manage to slip in under it

NOW

that you've read this
it's ok to turn the page

ECONOMIC CRISIS

buy low
stay high

LOVE
thank you
call again

LAMENT

I am not now
nor have I ever been

SOME DAYS
death
crosses my mind

WAY TO GO

gone

ON TIME

we become late
too soon

LIFE

here now
then not

REINCARNATION

here now
and then again

NOT THE BIRD

but the shadow of the bird

flying

NOW
soon to be
long ago

OUR HOUR
so short we long
for more

MY POEMS

so short we long
for more

QUANTUM POEM

here now and there now
unless you peek

REMEMBER ME
humorously
posthumously

REMEMBER
me

I
forget

IT
matters

NOTHING

can replace poetry in my life
and one day surely it will

JUST AS YOU ARE ABOUT TO GRASP IT

it's over

ABSENCE

neither here
nor there

THERE IS
no that
there

THERE IS

no more

THIS PAGE

intentionally
left blank